Ants

TEXT BY ELAINE PASCOE

PHOTOGRAPHS BY DWIGHT KUHN

BLACKBIRCH PRESS, INC.

WOODBRIDGE, CONNECTICUT

Published by Blackbirch Press, Inc.
260 Amity Road
Woodbridge, CT 06525

To my sister, Phyllis To Jean
–D.K. –E.P.

Email: staff@blackbirch.com
Web site: www.blackbirch.com

Printed in the United States

10 9 8 7 6 5 4 3 2 1

front cover: adult ant drinking from dew
back cover: (left to right) ant eggs, ant larvae, ant pupae, adult ant

Library of Congress Cataloging-in-Publication Data
Pascoe, Elaine.
Ants / by Elaine Pascoe. — 1st ed.
    p.   cm. — (Nature close-up)
    Includes bibliographical references (p. 47) and index.
    Summary: Describes the physical characteristics, habitats, and life cycle of ants. Includes related activities.
    ISBN 1-56711-183-1 (library binding : alk. paper)
    1. Ants—Juvenile literature. [1. Ants. 2. Ants—Experiments. 3. Experiments.] I. Title.
II. Series: Pascoe, Elaine. Nature close-up.
QL568.F7P36   1999   97-43571
595.79'6—dc21   CIP
                                                        AC

Note on metric conversions: The metric conversions given in Chapters 2 and 3 of this book are not always exact equivalents of U.S. measures. Instead, they provide a workable quantity for each experiment in metric units. The abbreviations used are:

cm	centimeter	**kg**	kilogram
m	meter	**l**	liter
g	gram	**cc**	cubic centimeter

CONTENTS

1

Ants All Over

No matter where you live, ants are nearby. They live in the freezing north, the blazing tropics, dry deserts, steamy jungles, and everywhere in between. They nest in the soil, in trees, under cracks in city pavement, and even in the timbers of houses. In their search for food they travel through meadows, forests, farm fields, and even into kitchen cupboards!

Ants have lived on Earth for more than 100 million years. While many other kinds of animals have lost the contest for survival and died out, ants have thrived. Today they are among the most widespread and interesting insects.

Ants are social insects; that is, they live in large groups, or colonies. Ant colonies are highly organized, complex societies, in which every ant has a job. Some of the things they do are truly amazing. There are ants that grow their own food, tend insect "cattle," and keep slaves! Like ants, people are also social beings. Perhaps that's why we find ants so fascinating.

An ant "milks" a treehopper that is guarding its recently laid eggs. "Milking" is a process where an ant takes liquid that is secreted by another insect.

ANT FACTS

If you could gather all the ants on Earth and weigh them, their combined weight would equal the combined weight of all the world's people! At least, that's what scientists estimate. No one really knows how many ants there are on Earth. About 4,500 different kinds, or species, have been identified. The greatest variety live in tropical rain forests, and there may be kinds there that have not yet been discovered.

Ants range from tiny species so small that they are difficult to see, to monsters well over an inch (2.5 cm) long. Large or small, however, ants share certain characteristics. Like all insects, ants have six legs and three main body parts—the head, thorax, and abdomen. Instead of an internal skeleton, they have a hard shell, or exoskeleton. They breathe through small holes called spiracles in the thorax and abdomen.

Top: An ant collects nectar from a brightly colored flower. *Bottom:* The world's largest ant, Dinoponera gigantea, can grow to longer than 1 inch (2.5 cm).

An ant's long antennae can sense information about scent, taste, temperature, wetness, and texture.

Two long antennae, attached to the head, are an ant's main way of getting information about the world around it. An ant waves its antennae in the air, taps them on the ground, and touches objects with them. The antennae pick up scents and tastes, as well as information about temperature, wetness, and texture. They help an ant find its way, locate food, and communicate with other ants through scent signals.

With such sensitive antennae, ants don't need good eyesight. Some ants are blind or nearly blind, with primitive eyes that can detect little more than light and dark. Others have large compound eyes that send multiple images to the ant's very tiny brain.

An ant's jaws are used for more than chewing food. Ants actually have two sets of jaws. The outer jaws, or mandibles, are powerful tools with sharp edges. Ants use them for digging, biting, carving, cutting, and holding food. But they can also use them gently, to move their young within the nest. The inner jaws have fine combs that are used to clean antennae and legs. Ants clean their antennae constantly with these combs and with a set of brushes on their front legs.

An ant's outer jaws are called mandibles.

An ant's legs have tiny claws that allow it to walk over many surfaces. Here, a nurse ant carries a pupa to a new location in its nest.

Tiny claws at the tip of an ant's legs help it crawl across all kinds of surfaces—even smooth walls. The claws grasp crevices and bumps that are too small for us to see— that's why ants sometimes seem to defy gravity by walking straight up a wall or upside down on the ceiling. At some stages of life, certain ants have wings. Like the legs, the wings attach to the thorax.

9

Unlike a termite (*inset*), an ant has a very thin waist that leads to the abdomen.

A narrow "waist" behind the thorax is a feature that sets ants apart from similar insects, such as termites. Behind it, in the abdomen, are two stomachs—one to digest food, and one to hold food in liquid form. An ant uses this second stomach, or crop, to carry food back to its colony, where it feeds other ants.

Female ants have a wand-like organ called an ovipositor at the tip of the abdomen. It is designed for egg laying, but in some species it's also a stinger. No male ants have stingers, but some types of ants inject poison with their bites. Others spray a harsh-smelling liquid at their enemies.

ADAPTABLE ANTS

One reason ants have been able to survive for millions of years is that they have been able to adapt to all sorts of conditions. Different types of ants may look alike, and they may all live in colonies, but they vary greatly in what they eat, how they obtain food, and where and how they nest. Ants are sometimes divided into groups based on these "lifestyle" differences.

Cattle tenders: Many ants collect honeydew, a sweet substance produced by tiny insects called aphids. To make sure that the colony will have a constant supply of honeydew, some ant species keep herds of aphids, tending them like milk cows. These ants capture aphids and put them out to "pasture" on plant stems. The aphids suck the plant juices and secrete honeydew, which the ants collect. Some ants shelter their aphids overnight. In cold climates, ants have been known to take aphid eggs into their nests for safekeeping through winter.

Honeypots: Yellow-brown honey ants store honeydew or sweet plant sap in a unique way—some members of the colony are actually living containers. These ants are fed honeydew until their abdomens are so swollen that they can't walk. Other ants in the colony can always get a meal by tapping a "honeypot." In Mexico, people consider these ants a sweet treat!

Harvesters: Harvester ants survive lean times by setting aside large stockpiles of seeds and grains. These ants collect the seeds, strip off their husks, and store them underground.

A "cattle tender" ant collects honeydew from a group of aphids.

Slave keepers: Several kinds of ants keep ant "slaves." Amazon ants—large red ants that live in the western United States—raid nests of black ants and steal their young. The Amazons carry the young back to their own nest and raise them. When they mature, the kidnapped ants become slaves, gathering food and feeding the Amazons.

Carpenters: Carpenter ants nest in wood. They use their powerful jaws to carve out tunnels and chambers. But these big black ants do not eat wood—their diet consists of other insects, rotting fruit, and other plant material. When they nest in house timbers, rather than the rotting trees that are their natural homes, they can do enormous damage.

Hunters: Many kinds of ants prey on other insects. The most dangerous hunters are army ants, which live in tropical regions. These meat-eating ants travel in huge columns. They swarm over the ground, devouring insects, spiders, beetles, even snakes, lizards, and small birds.

Top: A slave-keeper queen attacks another queen whose nest will be raided for slaves. *Bottom:* A carpenter ant with pupae inside a decaying log.

WATCH OUT! RED FIRE ANTS!

Red fire ants, originally found in South America, have become a major pest in the southern United States. These ants can inflict painful bites and stings. They first appeared in the United States in the 1940s, and since then they have spread through millions of acres. Only cold weather stops them—they can't live where winter temperatures drop below 10 degrees F (-12.2 degrees C).

Fire ants look like common red or red-brown ants, a quarter of an inch (0.6 cm) long or less. Their mounds, which are often quite large, can be seen in meadows, farm fields, and other open areas. The ants eat plants as well as insects and other small animals, which they kill with their venom. When lots of fire ants attack, they may kill larger animals, even pigs and calves.

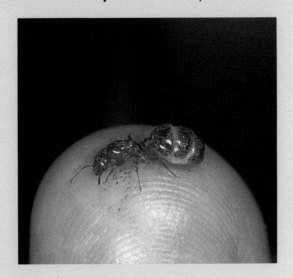

For most people, a fire ant sting is painful but not serious. But some people are especially sensitive or allergic to the venom. If these people receive many stings, and do not get medical help, they may die. It's best to stay clear of these ants and their mounds.

Farmers: Leaf-cutter ants of Central and South America grow their own food. The ants carry pieces of leaves to their nest, chew them up, and store them underground. Eventually, a fungus grows on the leaf material, providing food for the entire colony.

Other ants: Among the many other unusual ants are the bulldog ants of Australia, which are over an inch (2.5 cm) long. They can leap a foot (30 cm) into the air and deliver a nasty bite—and they will chase intruders for up to 30 feet (9 m) if their nests are disturbed.

ALL FOR ONE

No matter where or how big it is, an ant colony revolves around a single ant: the queen. With rare exceptions, she is the only member of the colony that lays eggs. All of the colony's members are her offspring. Everything they do is geared to ensuring her well-being and the survival of the colony. Even through cold winters, when the ants are dormant, the queen comes first. The ants cluster in the nest in a huge ball around her, protecting her and keeping her warm.

Nurse ants cluster around the much larger queen in the center.

Ants communicate important information to each other by touching mouths and antennae. Among other things, ants will tell each other where to find food.
Inset: Hunter ants collect food for the colony. Here an ant prepares to carry back to its nest praying mantis nymphs hatching from their egg case.

A soldier ant protects its nest and attacks a grasshopper that accidentally landed there.

The world outside the nest is a dangerous place for an ant. Birds, beetles, lizards, spiders, and other insect-eaters lie in wait. But an ant's worst enemies are often other ants. Besides slave raiders, there are ants that hunt and eat other ants. An ant that wanders too close to a strange nest may be killed, and sometimes battles break out between neighboring colonies.

If an ant doesn't fall victim to an enemy, it may live as long as 10 years. Queens have been known to live 20 years. But no ant can live long alone. Ants depend on all the other members of their colony to survive. That is partly why ants are known as some of the most social and cooperative insects in the natural world.

An ant falls prey to a grass spider that has created a trap in its dew-covered, sticky web.

ANTS AND PEOPLE

In homes and on farms, ants are pests. They steal food and damage crops. When carpenter ants invade a wooden building, they can do serious damage to the structure. Ants that bite and sting, such as fire ants, are especially unwelcome.

But ants are also helpful—even though people may not always be aware of the good things they do. They are part of the natural clean-up crew that disposes of dead animals and plant material. Many ants kill harmful insects. By tunneling in the ground to build their nests, ants help to improve the soil, keeping it loose and well aerated by allowing air and water to get in.

This ant colony established itself in a wooden structure.

A MODEL OF COOPERATION

People often compare ant society to human society. An ant colony is a model of cooperation, in which every member works for the good of the whole. In the way they store food and care for their young, some ants almost seem to be planning for the future. That's the idea behind the fable of the grasshopper and the ants, in which a careless grasshopper fiddles the summer away while ants busily prepare for the harsh winter to come. In fact, ants don't think about cooperation, or the future, or about much of anything. They act on instinct, which means they are biologically "programmed" to do the things they do. All the same, there's much to discover and learn by watching these fascinating insects.

An ant carries a grasshopper wing back to its colony.

2

Collecting and Caring for Ants

Ants are so common it is almost impossible to avoid them. But few people actually take time to observe their ways. You can learn a lot about these insects by watching them in nature, and by setting up an ant colony at home, for close observation.

You can buy a complete colony—including ants and a nest in which to keep and observe them—from biological supply firms, such as those listed on page 47. With patience and care, and perhaps some help from a parent or teacher, you can also collect wild ants and place them in a home that you make yourself.

This chapter will tell you where to look for ants, how to collect them, and how to set up both a temporary nest and a more permanent home. Remember that some ants can bite or sting. Fire ants are especially fierce—you should stay away from their nests. Regional Cooperative Extension offices and biology teachers may have information on the kinds of ants in your area. Seek help in identifying ants from knowledgeable grown-ups. Although there are exceptions, it is usually good to avoid red ants and to choose black or dark brown types instead— such as garden and carpenter ants.

25

ANT HUNT

Start your ant hunt almost anywhere—in a city park, in your yard, in woods or fields—in spring, summer, or fall. Take along a magnifying glass for observing the insects in the wild. Because ants are small and fragile (and because some bite or sting) it's best not to pick them up with your fingers. Bring a small garden trowel, a spoon, and a small paintbrush to collect them with. To carry ants home, take a plastic container covered with mesh, secured by a rubber band. Or use a zip-top plastic vegetable bag—the kind that has tiny holes in it, to let air in.

You may find ant hills, mounds of loose soil that mark the entrances of ant nests. Not all nests lie under ant hills, however. Some ants nest under flat stones—especially stones that are in the sun. The stone holds the sun's warmth, keeping the temperature in the nest even and warm. Carpenter ants nest in rotting wood. Look for little piles of sawdust by a fallen tree, signs that these carvers have been at work.

Can't find an ant nest? Look for ants. Sometimes the entrance to a nest is hidden by leaves or other debris. When you see a lot of ants coming and going, you are probably near a nest or a food source. Try to follow them to their nest.

A zip-top bag with holes in it is a perfect way to transport ants.

You can collect more ants by digging into an actual nest.

Ants move fast, and you will have to move fast to catch them. Using the paintbrush, brush them gently onto the spoon, and then quickly but carefully put them in the container. Be sure to close the container securely. Ants are excellent climbers, and they will find their way out through even the tiniest gap. Keep the container out of direct sunlight.

If you want to set up an ant colony at home, you may want to collect more than a few ants. Using a trowel or a spoon, gently dig into the nest to collect eggs, larvae, and pupae as well as workers. Put a small amount of nesting material in the container with the ants. Collect the queen if you find her—she will be the biggest ant. If you don't have the queen, your colony can still survive because workers will carry on raising the young.

27

ANT HOMES

If you plan to observe your ants for just a day or two, you can keep them in a small container, such as a clear plastic sandwich box. Put some slightly moistened sand or loose soil in the bottom. Add a few flat stones for the ants to hide under. Cover the top with clear plastic in which you've punched many small holes, to let in air. Secure the covering tightly with rubber bands.

If you want to watch the ants for a longer time, put them in an artificial nest. You can buy one of these "ant farms" or make your own. Here is a simple way:

What to Do:

1. Put the small bottle inside the large one, and fill the space between them with moist sand or soil. Leave some room at the top of the container.
2. Put your ants and any nesting material you collected on top of the sand.
3. Cover the container with mesh, and fasten the cover with rubber bands.

   Because the small bottle is in the center of the container, the ants will tunnel around the sides, where you can see them. You can encourage them to stay close to the sides by covering the container with a towel or dark material when you aren't watching them.

What You Need:

* Two sheets of clear Plexiglas™, about 12 inches (30 cm) square. Ask the hardware store to cut the pieces and sand the edges
* Two pieces of wood, 1-1/2 × 1-1/2 × 12 inches (4 × 4 × 30 cm), for the sides of the container
* One piece of wood, 1-1/2 × 1-1/2 × 9 inches (4 × 4 × 23 cm), for the base
* Two pieces of plywood, about 3 × 6 inches (8 × 15 cm)
* 3-inch (8-cm) screws or nails
* 3/4-inch (2-cm) screws or nails
* Black plastic electrical tape
* Duct tape
* Sand or sandy oil
* Mesh fabric or screening
* Rubber bands

You can also make a thin, clear-sided ant home.

What to Do:

1. Screw or nail the wood side pieces to the ends of the base.

2. Cover one edge of each Plexiglas™ sheet with black electrical tape. This will be the top edge.

3. Place one Plexiglas™ sheet on either side of the wooden frame, taped edges up. Use duct tape to hold the sheets onto the frame.

4. Add sand or sandy soil. You can help the ants get started by making some tunnels for them. For this, tip the container flat on one side and remove the top Plexiglas™ panel. Make your tunnels, and retape the panel.

5. Screw the plywood rectangles to the sides of the frame, so that the container will stand up. Put in your ants and cover the container with mesh fabric or screening held in place by rubber bands. With mesh, you may need to use tape to keep it secure.

CARING FOR ANTS

Before you transfer your ants to a new home, place them in the refrigerator for about an hour. Like all insects, ants are more active in warm temperatures. The cold temperature in the refrigerator will slow them down and make it easier for you to move them. All the same, it's a good idea to make the switch outdoors, if you can. That way, if some ants escape, they won't be in your house.

Most ants like a varied diet. Offer them small pieces of potato or apple, scraps of meat, crumbs of bread and cereal, and perhaps a few drops of honey or sugar water, or a sugar cube. Put the food on small pieces of cardboard or on leaves, and place it on top of the sand in the ant container. Don't give the ants too much food, and replace uneaten food with fresh food before it spoils—at least every other day.

Provide water by placing a piece of water-soaked sponge in the container. Moisten the sponge every day. If the sand begins to dry out, mist the surface lightly with water.

Keep your ants out of direct sunlight, which would make their container too warm. Ants that you collected in the wild can be released where you found them when you have finished watching them. Don't release ants that you buy. If they aren't native to your area, they may not survive—or they may become harmful pests.

You can feed ants a varied diet that includes fruit, vegetables, grains, and water.

Investigating Ants

This chapter contains some activities that will help you learn more about ants. You can use ants that you have collected for all of these activities. Several activities can also be done with free ants, follow the instructions in Chapter 2 for locating them. Remember to stay away from fire ants and other biting, stinging types.

WHAT DO ANTS LIKE TO EAT?

What foods do you think ants prefer? Make a prediction based on what you know about ants. Then find out if you are right by doing this activity. You can use wild ants or ants that you have collected.

What to Do:

1. Put equal amounts of each food on a piece of cardboard or leaf.
2. Place the cardboard or leaf in your ant home, or on the ground near an ant nest. On a windy day outdoors, anchor it with stones. Wait for ants to find the food.

Results: See which foods the ants eat first. (Outside, other insects or birds may come along and eat the foods, so you'll need to keep a close watch.)

Conclusions: What do your results tell you about the foods ants like? Try this activity again, using different foods. Or place the foods near the nest of a different type of ant. Are the results the same?

What You Need:
* Various foods—candy, cookies, lettuce, carrots, berries, honey, and so on
* Cardboard or leaves on which to put the foods

What You Need:

* Cookies, such as sugar wafers. Buy the cookies in various colors, or color them yourself with drops of food coloring
* Cardboard or leaves, on which to place the food

DOES SIZE OR COLOR AFFECT ANTS' FOOD CHOICES?

People like their food to look good, as well as taste and smell good. What about ants? Based on what you've read about these insects, decide what you think. Then test your answer with this experiment, using free ants or ants that you have collected.

What to Do:

1. Break a cookie into several pieces, ranging in size from big chunks to tiny crumbs. Put the pieces on a piece of cardboard or leaf.

2. Place the cardboard or leaf in your ant home, or on the ground near an ant nest. Wait for ants to find it.

3. Set up the experiment again, using cookies of several different colors. Break off one small piece from each cookie, making the pieces all the same size.

Results: Check often to see which pieces ants head for first.

Conclusions: Was your prediction correct? Repeat the activity, switching the position of the food pieces on the cardboard. Do you get the same results?

38

WHAT DO ANTS LIKE TO DRINK?

Like all living things, ants need water to survive. In nature, they get liquids from dew that forms at night, in food, and from other sources. Decide what kinds of liquids you think ants prefer, and then do this activity with wild ants or ants that you have collected.

What to Do:

1. Put a drop of each liquid on the leaf or piece of cardboard. The drops should be the same size.
2. Place the leaf or cardboard in your ant home, or on the ground near an ant nest. Wait for ants to find it.

Results: See which liquids the ants choose.

Conclusion: What do your results tell you about how ants prefer to get water?

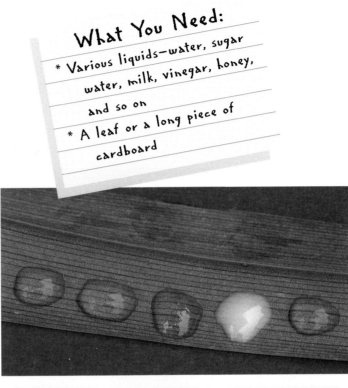

What You Need:
* Various liquids—water, sugar water, milk, vinegar, honey, and so on
* A leaf or a long piece of cardboard

What You Need:

* Ants in an ant home, as described in Chapter 2
* A sheet of dark construction paper, or dark cloth
* A sheet of white paper
* Tape

WOULD ANTS RATHER TUNNEL IN LIGHT OR DARKNESS?

Ants are always working on their nests, enlarging and repairing the tunnels and chambers. Do you think they'd prefer to do this work in the dark or in the light? Decide what you think, and then do this experiment to find out.

What to Do:

1. Tape dark construction paper or cloth over one third of the ant farm. It will keep light from entering that section.
2. Tape white paper over another third. It will filter out some, but not all, the light. Leave the rest of the surface uncovered.
3. Put the ant farm in a bright, but not sunny, spot. In a few days, remove the paper and see where the ants have tunneled.

Results: In which section do you see the most tunnels?

Conclusion: Why do you think ants built tunnels where they did?

IN WHAT MATERIALS DO ANTS PREFER TO BUILD TUNNELS?

Ants build nests anywhere, but some places are more suitable than others. Based on what you've read, make a prediction about the type of soil ants like best. Then test your prediction with this activity.

What to Do:

1. Set up this activity outdoors, in case some ants escape as you move them. Begin by filling the jars with different materials. Put dry sand in one, slightly damp sand in the second, a slightly damp mixture of sand and soil in the third, slightly damp soil in the fourth, and wet, soggy soil in the fifth.

What You Need:

* Ants
* Five clear, wide-mouthed pint or quart jars, such as canning jars
* Sand
* Garden soil
* An aquarium, plastic storage box, or similar container, big enough to hold all five jars
* Mesh, to cover the large container
* Rubber bands and tape

2. Put the jars, uncovered, in the large container. Add a piece of damp sponge, to provide water, and ant foods, as described in Chapter 2.

3. Place the ants in the container and cover it with mesh. Fasten the mesh tightly with rubber bands and tape.

4. Put the container in a sheltered place, out of direct sunlight. Care for the ants as described in Chapter 2.

Results: Watch the ants to see which jar they tunnel in.

Conclusion: What do your results tell you about the kinds of places that tunneling ants might choose for their nests?

MORE ANT ACTIVITIES

1. Find an ant nest outside, and observe the ants as they go back and forth. Take a magnifying glass so you can get a close look at them. When two ants meet, what do they do?

2. After you've watched for a while, you'll probably notice that ants come and go from the nest along the same routes, or ant trails. Follow one of these trails away from the nest. Then, using a spoon and brush as described in Chapter 2, pick up an ant and move it off the trail. Carry it several yards in any direction, and gently set it down. Watch the ant to see what it does. How does it find its way back?

3. Find an ant of a different species or another insect, such as a grasshopper, and place it on the nest (or in your ant home, if you have collected ants). What do the ants do? Watch their reactions for ten minutes or so, and write a description of what you have seen.

4. Remove an ant from its colony for several days. Keep the ant in a temporary home, as described in Chapter 2, and don't forget to give the ant food and water. How does it behave when it's alone? What happens when you return it to the colony?

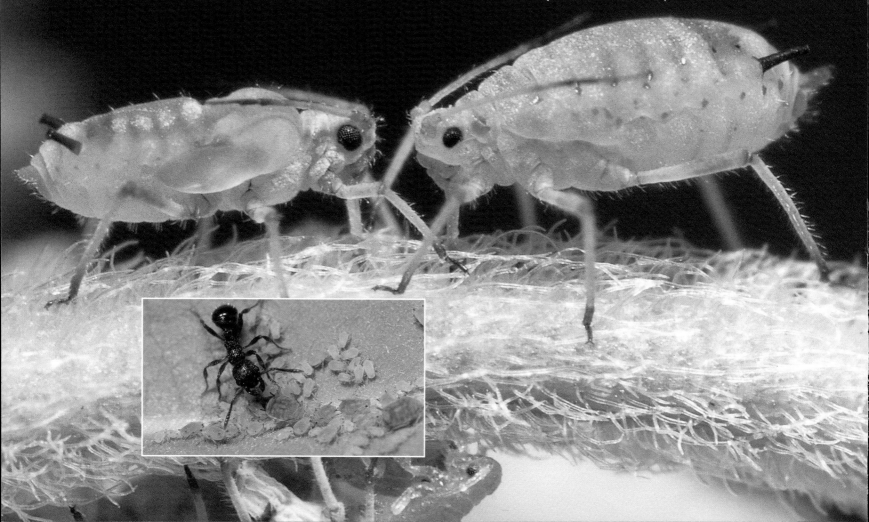

5. Look for aphids on leaves and stems in gardens and grass. These tiny insects often cluster on the undersides of leaves. A magnifying glass will help you get a good look at them. You may see ants climbing on the plant with the aphids. Watch to see if the ants "milk" the aphids, stroking them to prompt them to release the sweet liquid called honeydew.

Two aphids stand on a milkweed stem. *Inset:* A black ant milks aphids for their honeydew.

RESULTS AND CONCLUSIONS

Here are some possible results and conclusions for the activities on pages 37 through 42. Many factors may affect the outcomes of these activities—the types of ants you use, the type of home you set up for them, and other conditions. If your results differ, try to think of reasons why. Repeat the activity with different conditions, and see if your results change.

What Do Ants Like to Eat?

Most ants love sweets, so you'll probably see them heading for the cookies, candy, honey, and similar foods.

Does Size or Color Affect Ants' Food Choices?

With their sensitive antennae, ants are drawn to smells and tastes. They have poor sight and care little about color, and their strong jaws let them nibble on cookie chunks of any size.

What Do Ants Like to Drink?

Ants will usually head for sweet liquids, such as sugar water and honey. Besides providing water, these liquids provide nourishment.

Would Ants Rather Tunnel in Light or Darkness?

You'll probably see the most tunnels in the darkest part of the nest. Ants avoid light, and they don't need it to work—they rely almost entirely on touch and scent.

In What Materials Do Ants Prefer to Build Tunnels?

You'll probably find that ants avoid very wet soil, but otherwise they aren't very choosy.

45

SOME WORDS ABOUT ANTS

dormant: Inactive.

exoskeleton: The hard outer skin of an insect. It takes the place of an internal skeleton.

instinct: An inborn, automatic response.

larvae: The young of ants. They look like tiny grubs or worms.

ovipositor: A tube, extending from the back of the abdomen, that ant queens use to lay eggs, and that females of some species use as a stinger.

pupae: Ant young in a dormant state, maturing into adults.

spiracles: Holes through which ants breathe.

SOURCES FOR ANTS AND SUPPLIES

You can buy ants and artificial ant nests through the mail. If you obtain insects through mail-order sources such as those listed here, do not release them into the wild.

Carolina Biological Supply
2700 York Road
Burlington, NC 27215
(800) 334-5551

Connecticut Valley Biological
82 Valley Road, P.O. Box 326
Southampton, MA 01073
(800) 628-7748

Insect Lore
P.O. Box 1535
Shafter, CA 93263
(800) LiveBug

FOR FURTHER READING

Chinery, Michael. *Life Story Ant*. Mahwah, NJ: Troll, 1991.

Fischer-Nagel, Heiderose and Andreas. *An Ant Colony*. Minneapolis, MN: Carolrhoda, 1989.

Greenland, Caroline. *Ants*. Danbury, CT: Grolier, 1986.

Parramon, J. M. *The Fascinating World of Ants*. Hauppauge, NY: Barron, 1991.

INDEX

Note: Page numbers in italics indicate pictures.

Photo Credits

Page 6 (bottom): © Paul A. Zahl/Photo Researchers, Inc.; page 12 (top): © Gregory G. Dimijian/Photo Researchers, Inc.; page 13: © Penn State Entomology/Photo Researchers, Inc.